Small Town Dream
The Guide for Moving to Small Town America

By
Andrew LaPointe
Copyright 2018

Edited by Kim Schneider

www.SmallTownDream.com

Small Town Dream is available at special quantity discounts to use as premiums and sales promotions. Small Town Dream makes great closing gifts and giveaways for real estate agents, title insurance companies and anyone involved in real estate, moving companies, relocation services, etc.

For more information, please call 1-877-746-7477 or visit www.SmallTownDream.com and contact us.

All rights reserved. No portion of this book may be used or reproduced in any manner without written permission.

The information in this publication does not constitute a recommendation to move to small town America. The publisher and the author are not engaged in rendering investment advisory, real estate, legal, tax or accounting advice. If such assistance is required, seek the advice of a professional.

Please Note: This book is meant for educational and informational purposes only. The material in this book is general information and is designed to educate and not make individual recommendations. It would be impossible to provide detailed information about every small town in America. Thus, it is assumed the reader has a general idea of the area or region of Small Town America they would like to move to. Taking this assumption into consideration, this book was written to help the reader to make that dream a reality. It is not meant to provide specific information on property taxes, weather patterns, road conditions, etc. You can use the information in this book as a guide to help you to make a decision to move to any location you desire.

The reader is solely responsible for making his or her own assessment of the material in this book. Individual results may vary. The author and the publisher shall not be held liable for any loss or liability or damage which may occur as a result of any individual acting upon the educational information in this book.

This book is not a recommendation to move to small town America. Neither the author nor the publisher assumes any responsibility for any errors or omissions. The publisher and the author are not engaged in rendering investment advisory, real estate, legal, tax or accounting advice. If such assistance is required, seek the advice of a professional.

This book is not about selling everything you own and relocating to a small town. Such an action would be irresponsible. Be very careful when making such a life changing decision. Consult a competent professional to discuss your individual situation.

Acknowledgements:

To my wife Jennifer, for sharing my life and my Small Town Dream.

Special thanks to all the people in the all places I have been who asked me how I could live where I do and inspired me to write this book. A lifetime of appreciation to my parents for all of the precious moments and fond memories. You not only made my childhood happy, you also created a legacy that my children and hopefully their children will share.

"Live your dreams and believe in yourself.
That is the only way to the top."

- Andrew LaPointe

Small Town Dream – The Guide to Moving to Small Town America

Contents

Introduction	5
Migration from City to Modern-Rural Areas (Small Town America)	9
"The Small Town Dream"	11
Does Employment Exist?	14
Creating your Small Town Dream Goals	18
Lifetime Goals	20
Live Life on Your Own Terms	21
A Story About Other People's Opinions and Criticisms	23
How to Reposition Your Life to Follow Your Lifetime Goals	25
Getting Started: Follow Your Dreams	25
Do Whatever it Takes	27
Four Fundamental Steps You Must Take Before Moving to Small Town America	28
Create a Family Policy Statement	29
Focus: It's the Reason Why You Set Goals	37
Research Your Goals	38
Fifteen Strategies to Smooth Your Transition and Validate Your Family Policy Statement	38
A Lifestyle or a Job…It's Your Choice	48
Monthly Cash Flow Statement	51
Create a Monthly Budget Allocation	55
Monthly Transaction Record Sheets	56
Monthly Transaction Record Sheets	58
Create an Emergency Fund	60
The Debt Elimination Pyramid	67
Debt Elimination Pyramid Worksheet	70
How to Stop Using Your Credit Cards	72
How to Make Money in a Small Town	74
Career Action Plan Worksheet	77
Small Town Success Story	79
Getting Ready to Move to Your Small Town	96
A Road Map for Success	98
Small Town Preparation List	98
10½ Step Small Town Dream Checklist	101
Contact List	105

Small Town Dream – The Guide to Moving to Small Town America

Introduction

Since I was 8 years old, I remember my parents packing up the camper and driving my brothers, sisters and me to a small town in Northern Michigan. Back then the five-hour drive from the Detroit suburb of Taylor to Northern Michigan seemed to take forever.

We kids were excited about the prospect of exploring new destinations, and my parents enjoyed every minute of the open road. Over the years of my youth, we roamed the back roads of America in the family Winnebago and visited every tourist trap our great country had to offer. We traveled from Michigan to Oregon, from Ohio to the Carolinas, and Florida to the Dakotas. I learned firsthand about the encompassing beauty of America and the importance of family vacations. During those early days, I fell in love with the small towns we visited.

As I grew older, I traveled to many cities of our great nation but had yet to experience the unique lifestyle offered by small town America. To a young adult, big cities seem to offer everything the heart desires: the ability to dine in world-class restaurants and enjoy first-rate entertainment and the convenience of having all of these amenities within a short walking distance. Yet, with all of the modern experiences offered by the big-city, the small town is the only place where I ended up feeling truly relaxed and at home.

In fact, for first time in some 200 years more people are moving to smaller, rural areas than are moving to the big city. And the places to which they're moving are regions populated by small towns—places where people enjoy holiday seasons as if they lived in a Norman Rockwell painting, where recreational amenities abound, and where incidentally, you can find more and more big-city amenities, say a sushi bar next door to the small-town hardware. If you think living the small town dream sounds like paradise, keep reading. This book is for you.

Turn Your Small Town Dreams into Goals

Obstacles are those frightful things you see when you take
your eyes off your goal.
~ Henry Ford ~

Nearly every major metropolitan area has an escape hatch for its residents. The East Coast offers the Jersey shore and the Atlantic beaches. The West Coast has Napa Valley, Las Vegas, the Rocky Mountains and the Pacific Ocean. The Midwest offers crystal clear lakes and countless golf courses.

History offer numerous examples of families from all walks of life escaping the heat of the city to enjoy a few short days enjoying small town America. Like many small towns across our great land, the small towns of Northern Michigan, for example, have attracted some of the world's richest families including the Fords, the Edisons and the Firestones. It also entertained the likes of Al Capone and Bugsy Malone, some of the roughest characters of the roaring 20s.

With the birth and expansion of major metropolitan suburbs since the 1800s, small town America continues to inspire and relax countless millions. From lush green forests to crystal clear lakes, many small towns are truly magical. In addition, most offer everything from wide-open blue skies to beautiful sugar-sand beaches without losing the ability to enjoy all of the amenities of modern life.

For many, small town America is perfectly designed to speak to the inner needs of human existence. The small town lifestyle offers inner peace and personal reflection. The serene surroundings permit you to reflect upon the most important factors of your life. Spending time in the small town of your choosing allows you to clear your mind and prioritize your goals and dreams thus creating a more focused and enjoyable life.

Whether you are driving along a cherry orchard in full bloom or strolling downtown past the neighborhood pharmacy, you find yourself noticing the small treasures of life, such as the laughter of children, seagulls floating on the wind or snow-white clouds afloat in a clear blue sky.

When you slow down and take your time, the small town lifestyle can help shed light on what really matters in life. You'll forget about the traffic jams back home or the daily commute and find that inner peace that only comes when you take time to reflect on what really matters to you and your family. Once you find that inner peace, you'll never want to let it go.

Everyone who has ever headed back to the big city from a small town weekend getaway wishing that they didn't have to leave knows exactly what I mean. When you reach this stage, it's time to starting planning your small town dream. This book will teach you that you can enjoy small town America as a full-time resident.

Ask yourself this. Do you want a lifestyle or a style-of-life? The difference is vast and, while most people settle for a style-of-life, there is an alternative.

A style-of-life is trying to enjoy the small town lifestyle in a short weekend getaway. With a style-of-life, you want to "experience" everything small town America has to offer in 48 hours because you have to rush back home and may not be back for another six months.

A small town lifestyle is what you get when small town America is your home. I call it the Small Town Dream. It's an opportunity to enjoy all the beauty your chosen small town has to offer—not in a day, but over your entire lifetime. It's the opportunity to see the stars of the Milky Way without looking though the overlay of big city lights. It's enjoying a relaxing walk along a stream on your own 5-acre parcel of property with your kids. As years pass and the memories grow, you'll truly understand that living the Small Town Dream is a lifestyle; it's not a vacation or weekend retreat.

The Small Town Dream enables you to live life on your terms. Many small towns offer everything from dance clubs and symphonies to world-class restaurants and shopping malls. No matter where you live, you can usually find everything you need within a relatively short drive from the small town you call home. Once you decide the small town lifestyle you desire for your family, you can find the small town to match your needs.

Small Town Dream – The Guide to Moving to Small Town America

Migration from City to Modern-Rural Areas (Small Town America)

Find out where the people are going and buy the land before they get there.
~ Will Rogers ~

A growing number of people of all ages are looking to plant roots in places not unlike the roots of America itself: the small town. They want what Thoreau called the " tonic of wildness" as part of the balance of daily life—one that includes more time with family, nature, and for spiritual reflection. More and more, they're finding that balance in small communities, looking there for a chance to make strong connections with neighbors and community and to shape the place in which they live.

According to the U.S. Department of Agriculture, Economic Research Services Urban Influence (2013), two population groups are reshaping the migration from the big city to rural America. The two population groups driving this movement are the young adults ages 20 to 34 and older adults 65 and older.

The younger generation is attracted to rural area rich in natural resources, while the older generation is attracted to areas that offer a wide selection of recreational activities. These activities can range from entertainment industries to natural resources including lakes, rivers and vacation-type destinations. Those folks from each generation are a mixed lot seeking remarkably similar things. Those things combine to make up what we refer to in this book as "the small town dream."

Rural areas in the Upper Great Lakes region were among the population "winners," as were the Mountain West, the Ozarks, part of the south and the rural Northeast—not surprising given the country's heritage in those quaint New England towns. Areas rich in recreational amenities and those considered retirement destination spots grew the most. What the population changes also show is that more young families and single professionals are seeking retirement amenities long before social security age.

In another study by Kenneth M. Johnson, a demographer and sociology professor at Loyola University-Chicago, and Calvin L. Beale, senior demographer at the U.S. Department of Agriculture's Economic Research Service. In their study "Rural Rebound," they found:

- The resettling of rural America is by a diversity of people.
    - The new arrivals are a mixed lot of retirees, blue-collar workers, entrepreneurs, and disenchanted city dwellers—all seeing a better way of life in small towns.

- More families with children are choosing to raise kids in the country.
    - The under-65 age group may be contributing more to rural migration than those over 65 as more people in their 30s, and their children, are moving to—or remaining in—rural areas.

- Migration to rural places isn't what it used to be.
    - Americans are not returning to a pioneering life of farming, though specialty farms are on the rise. They are using technology to "telecommute" to work several states or nations away, and new attitudes toward work are leading to models other than a 9-5 existence.

- Moving rural is not a romantic fixation.
    - While moves in the 1990s to small towns were thought to be about nostalgia, that doesn't seem to be the case today. More and more, people are consciously weighing many lifestyle factors and finding that cities don't necessarily offer the best jobs, the most security or the richest lifestyle. In addition, they're finding that streets are often dirtier, schools more dangerous and mortgages higher, the researchers found.

"The Small Town Dream"

You have to leave the city of your comfort and go into the wilderness of your intuition. What you'll discover will be wonderful. What you'll discover is yourself.
~ Alan Alda ~

The move to a small-town is not so much about a change of location as it is about changing a lifestyle, something this book will help you achieve—one step at a time.

The small town dream is about finding a career that complements and enables a certain lifestyle. It's about combining the best of big-city living with the simplicity of nature. For some, it's about skipping the stressful Sunday drive home from the weekend cottage and instead ending the workday at 3 p.m. for an afternoon of kayaking, sailing or skiing through the pines.

For others, it's about raising children who can spend their days hunting for rocks on the beach instead of sitting in front of a video game, who know the magic of listening to a pair of barred owls calling to each other in the woods. It's about feeling connected to something greater through the simple act of seeing a sky filled with stars. It's about returning to our roots.

America began as a small town. Although Boston and New York have skyscrapers and traffic congestion today, much of New England still is dotted with small towns. Why?

Maybe it is the history the area proudly captures, a history that represents a simpler time and simpler life and the ability to enjoy time with family, the outdoors and something larger than ourselves. Many aspects of our heritage were developed in small, rural towns. These are the places that feed the country, and much of the world, with countless varieties of foods. But they also seem to feed our spirits.

An anthropologist from the University of Michigan recently moved to Northern Michigan to examine why small towns are making such a comeback, and in particular why people are moving for reasons other than increasing their income or furthering a career. He's named the trend "lifestyle migration."

Dr. Brian Hoey spent more than a year conducting in-depth interviews with people who often gave up the security of big salaries and impressive titles to answer a call to a simpler life. What Hoey found is not necessarily what he expected. The migrants weren't just seeking simplicity in the sense of the back-to-land movement of the 1960s and 70s. Few were looking to farm the land. And they weren't for the most part into poverty or self-denial.

"It's about a deliberate or voluntary reordering of priorities," he said. People are asking what makes a life worth living and emphasizing those aspects of life in a new location more conducive to achieving them.

Hoey notes that the local Northern Michigan catch phrase, "A view of the bay is worth half the pay" was not generally spoken with frustration by his research subjects, but rather as a measure of personal pride. The phrase, he notes, "emphasizes the choice to live more in tune with the ideals of a quest for something more fulfilling than material gain."

To be sure, some lifestyle migrants find ways to incomes larger than those they left behind. Some telecommute to the same job, at the same salary, but save on commuting and wardrobe expenses. One former metropolitan television anchor will pass the $1 million in sales mark this year as a small-town bread maker.

And while he admits that he often works more hours than he used to, he feels life is more balanced. He can head out his front door for a hike on snowshoes through the woods, or head off hunting with his Springer spaniel.

For most, the small town dream is about gaining more control over life by being freed in some measure from an unpredictable economy. More people are living like the "artist" traditionally has, says Richard Florida, author of The Rise of the Creative Class.

They're looking to live life on their own terms and own schedules, managing their careers as a kind of free agent. More and more, they're looking to combine all aspects of their lives and are defining themselves by more than how they make their money: simultaneously being writer, researcher, consultant, cyclist, rock climber, wine enthusiast, microbrewer, gourmet cook. These people are not seeking to "get away from it all," but instead want to do it all and with their eyes wide open.

Where they want to do it all is in places that spark creativity: beautiful, natural environments that also have a dose of the hip: cafes and bistros, cultural events, places amenable to active recreation like biking, kayaking, trail running, snowboarding. Where those creative people go, Florida speculates, smart companies will follow.

Does Employment Exist?

All of our dreams can come true, if we have the courage to pursue them.
~ Walt Disney ~

Many dismiss their dream of living in a smaller town out of the mistaken notion that they'll be doomed to a life of poverty. They need to take a closer look. Small-town job options today go well beyond prospects like waiting tables at a local diner or working as a grass cutter all summer long.

Dramatic advances in technology mean that some of the nation's most remote communities are connected to the world through broadband and high-speed Internet access. And a growing number of companies are relocating their headquarters, manufacturing plants or call centers to small communities that offer big quality of life. Even still, finding a rewarding career in a small town takes a little creativity. You aren't likely to find your dream in the local classified ads.

To be sure, some jobs are in demand in smaller communities, and at a pay rate comparable to that in bigger cities. Health care and teaching are two prominent examples.

But as this book will show you, you need not be tied to a town's economy to make a good living. Telecommuting is becoming a viable option in a growing number of career fields. The "top" 10 careers from which you can work from home, according to The Center for the New West, are accounting, law, investment advising, marketing/public relations, business/management consulting, environmental consulting, political consulting, freelance writing, research, and software development.

In my region of Northern Michigan, its not uncommon to find people who teach correspondence courses in children's literature, write software for Internet sites, advise investment clients in New York City—all from home offices overlooking hardwood forests or inland lakes, perhaps with a few Alpaca wandering the yard.

A few converging trends are making these options more viable most anywhere:

- Better airport infrastructure and ability to commute via air travel. For example, you'll often find daily direct flights from small town America to corporate headquarters in the big city.

- Increasing availability (and affordability) of broadband and high speed Internet access.

- More people placing quality of life before career—and moving where they want to have their life—means companies are following to places where they can are finding creative employees ready and waiting.

- Community networking is easier in small towns. Entrepreneurs are building a community network for their small businesses and finding they can keep both production and business relationships local.

- The Internet means less isolation, wherever you may locate. High end shopping, or even courses toward a master's degree, are only a click away.

- Educational opportunities. Towns without a major university are offering increasing educational opportunities, through local school districts and community colleges. University centers are increasingly again popularity. A university center is collaboration between several major state universities offer degrees—including a master's and doctorate programs.

A recent survey of Fortune 500 companies that have located in small or mid-sized cities—and remained there from 20 to 130 years—found they developed a shared culture and identity and had fates strongly intertwined with the health of the community.

They did acknowledge some downsides: Sometimes limited options in housing, quality health care, culture, quality schools, employment options for spouses. But those were problems less often than you might think.

Local clinics are increasingly offering specialization, and experts in a surprising number of fields could be found in small towns. What these companies also found was a strong work ethic and low turnover of workers. The Internet helped alleviate isolation, and what small schools could offer in individual attention and opportunities for all kids to participate in sports and drama, for example, more than made up for what they lacked.

Many towns with populations between 10,000 to 50,000 support businesses and offer a quality of life that would be the envy of big-city executives and commuters, according to the group Partners for Livable Communities.

Each year, the group identifies resourceful, creative, beautiful communities—the most livable places in America. Recent winners include towns like Elkhart Indiana, population 45,000, where the proximity to University of Notre Dame provides plenty of cultural and recreational opportunities. You'll find wildlife sanctuaries and Amish communities and one of largest collections of Norman Rockwell paintings in the country. But you also won't have to starve to make a go of it. The town's home to multi billion dollar industries as among in RV and manufactured housing makers, and it's also known as the band instrument capitol of the world.

Salem, Massachusetts, one of the nation's original small towns, has a thriving business base you wouldn't expect in a town of 40,000—as well as its better-known coastal beauty. Fayetteville, Arkansas, a beautiful town at the foothills of the Ozarks, made the cut for recreational opportunities on its rivers and hiking and biking trails. The cost of living is 10 percent below the national average and employers based there include Wal Mart, J.B. Hunt and Tyson Foods and increasingly new companies attracted by a new technology center. Even the Northern Michigan town of Traverse City made this list. The cherry capitol of the world was twice named the top small town in America for business growth as well as one of the nation's best places to play golf or vacation with a family.

What all these communities have found is a careful balance between the built and natural environments, a creative energy that complements often stunning backwoods beauty.

And if there isn't a major employer like Wal Mart in the town you've chosen? Look to your own interests and needs and see if there's a niche you can fill. What do you as a consumer want but can't find? What product or service would make your life easier or more enjoyable? Do these exist where you want to locate? Would you enjoy filling that niche? Can't think of an original idea? Consider options popular in tourist-based economies like bed and breakfast operations, outfitting businesses or a specialty farm—even a combination of more than one. Just make sure you get excited about any possibilities that make your list. It may be cliché, but it's true: Do what you love and success will follow.

Creating your Small Town Dream Goals

Faith is taking the first step even when you don't see the whole staircase.
~ Martin Luther King, Jr. ~

Unless you're independently wealthy, the small town lifestyle you are envisioning may seem out of reach, just a dream that you'd love to see come true. To that I ask, "How badly do you want it?" Only you can answer that question, but time and time again, history has shown that people who know what they want and focus on their goals have achieved success more often than not.

Mountains are climbed. Rivers are conquered. Records are set. The man or woman of your dreams says, "I do." These achievements occur because one of the benefits of being human is our ability to choose among the many opportunities that present themselves each day and because somebody made a choice. Your small town dream is much the same. You can choose to pursue your small town dream or not. However, in the final moment of your life your choices will be no more. At the end of your life would you rather say, "I'm glad I did" or "I wish I would have?"

So how are great accomplishments achieved? In the moment of decision, you weigh the potential benefits of various courses of action against the potential costs. Some times the choices are between a course of action that offers the least amount of risk or the greatest amount of reward. Great accomplishments occur when the latter path is chosen. While not every decision we are faced with everyday is one that carries the weight of tremendous achievement, we all still strive to make decisions that will be the most beneficial to us and to those we love. So, with all the decisions you encounter every day, is there a secret to making the right one every time? Yes, there is.

The secret to making the right decision every time is to determine what will take you closer to your lifetime goal. Did you notice I wrote "lifetime goal" and not "long-term goal?" The difference between the two is vast. Long-term goals are things you would like to accomplish. Lifetime goals are things you must accomplish. These are goals that you want to achieve no matter what it takes.

One of the best ways to determine the difference between your lifetime goals and your long-terms goal is ask yourself the following question: "If I knew I was going to die one year from today, what would I want to accomplish?" One year is a very good length of time because it gives you the time you need to achieve your goals, yet it limits how much time you can waste. So, "What are your lifetime goals?"

Lifetime Goals

If you already have a list of lifetime goals waiting on the tip of your tongue, it's time to put them in ink. Writing down your goals is a time-tested tactic for the achievement of success that has been replicated by everyone from self-help guru Anthony Robbins to actor Jim Carrey. It worked for them. It can work for you.

If you don't already have a list of lifetime goals that you can rattle off at the drop of a hat, it's time to get one. Take your time and really think about the things that are important to you. When you've got your list, write it down and don't look at it for three days. When you see the list again, decide if there's anything that you want to change. Repeat the process until the goals on the list represent your lifetime goals.

For most people, housing choices play a large role in dictating lifestyle. Where you live has an enormous impact on your quality of life, your peace of mind and how your children will be raised. For an increasing number of people, the "Small Town Dream" is a lifetime goal.

Use the blank lines that follow to write your lifetime goals.

_____

_____

_____

_____

Prioritize Your Lifetime Goals

Now that you have a list of your lifetime goals, it's time to put your goals in order. Prioritizing your goals will help you determine if there are areas of your life that must be addressed first in order to make it possible to achieve your other goals. Write your prioritized list below:

1. _____

2. _____

3. _____

4. _____

5. _____

6. _____

Now that you have a list of your goals and you've prioritized them, the next step is to systematically work toward accomplishing them. If some of these goals seem far away right now, keep in mind that a million-mile journey begins with a single step. By writing down your goals, you have already taken the first step.

Live Life on Your Own Terms

Now that you have identified your true inner desires, how do you reposition your life so you can live your Small Town Dream? I will answer this question shortly, but first let's talk about the biggest obstacle you must overcome as soon as you decide to pursue your lifetime goal. Without a doubt, the biggest challenge you will face is dealing with the opinions and criticisms of others.

"Who does he think he is to quit his job and move to a small town?" you'll likely hear others say. "He has a wife and family to support. Why doesn't he just visit his lake house on weekends like everybody else?" or "She's 50 years old, she can't start a business. She can't just run off and do anything she wants to do."

Other people's opinions and criticisms arise anytime you do something that is outside the critic's comfort zone. If you're a skydiver, somebody will say, "That's dangerous." If you set out to write a book, somebody will say, "That's a waste of time." Other people's opinions and criticisms are like heavy chains that drag you down and hold you back from achieving your goals. If you listen to the critics, they will rob you of your happiness and stop you from reaching your goals.

A Story About Other People's Opinions and Criticisms

I once knew a widow named Henrietta who owned 20 acres of development real estate in addition to her primary residence. Her deceased husband's sister owned the neighboring 20-acre parcel.

Henrietta had always wanted a spiral staircase to the second story of her home. However, she and her husband never got around to building it. At the time we met, her husband had been deceased nearly five years, and Henrietta was thinking about selling her 20 acres and using the money to build her dream staircase (among other things).

When her children and her sister-in-law learned what she was considering, they made her life miserable. The children called her up almost every day and told her that they were entitled to the vacant property. Her sister-in-law called on the days her kids didn't and told her that she thought her brother would want the property to stay in the family.

The sister-in-law also told Henrietta that if she did sell it, it wouldn't be right for her to make a profit. The sister-in-law demanded it be sold to her at the original purchase price. The market price per acre was approximately $15,000, and the original cost was about $500 per acre.

Henrietta let these other people's opinions eat her up inside. The kids weren't interested in their mother's dreams of building a staircase and traveling; they were only waiting for their inheritance. The sister-in-law wanted the property so she could own the whole 40 acres. The market value of the entire 40-acre parcel would be worth over $500,000.

Since I lost touch with Henrietta, I never did learn whether she built her dream staircase or gave in to the pressure. The worst part of this story is that the complaints from Henrietta's critics originated from their own greed, discomfort, and insecurity. Remember when people criticize you, their comments usually stem from an unresolved issue within themselves. So don't worry what other people think, do, or say. Remember, it's your life, not theirs.

How to Reposition Your Life to Follow Your Lifetime Goals

Now that you have rediscovered your life passions, how do you reposition your life to follow your goals? The answer is simple, yet many won't do it. The answer: Do whatever it takes. If you absolutely know what your destiny is, the only person you can fail is yourself. Go for it!

Getting Started: Follow Your Dreams

After my wife Jennifer and I graduated from college, we moved to a small town in Northern Michigan. At that time, neither of us had a job. Jennifer was 22 years old, and I was 23. We had $500 in the bank and $5,000 in credit card debt. We moved on December 31, 1992. It was the worst day of the year to travel. The I-75 Expressway was covered with icy snow, and a howling blizzard poured sleet and freezing rain on us during the entire trip. At one point, the wind was so strong it pushed my pick-up truck off the road and into a snow bank. Fortunately, my truck and cargo were undamaged.

But our psyches were. We weren't even settled in yet and had started to reconsider our decision to move to a small Northern town. Would the winters always be this cruel? Would we need to buy a four-wheel drive truck? Had we made the wrong decision? These and many other questions raced through our minds as we inched our way north on I-75. Twenty years later, we wouldn't move from Northern Michigan for any reason. We love where we live, and we want our family to live in a small town for many generations to come.

When we moved, we didn't have jobs, we didn't have money, and we didn't have a plan; however, we did have a goal. The goal was simple. We wanted to build our future in the pristine beauty of Northern Michigan. Once we moved, our plan emerged—to put food on the table and a roof over our heads.

The first few years were the toughest because we were a young couple with credit card debt, car payments, and rent to pay. We worked many different jobs to make ends meet. At first, that was any job that paid the bills. My initial job was selling timeshare real estate at a local resort. Jennifer worked through a temporary employment agency as a secretary.

Since our bills were high and our income was low, we both moonlighted to keep food on the table. In addition to my day job, I mowed lawns, plowed driveways and shoveled snow off roofs. Jennifer worked nights as a bookkeeper. With all that, we had a combined income of approximately $28,000 during our first year.

A few years later, I chose to enhance my career. To reach this goal, I worked in another state Monday through Friday. I saw my wife and young family only on weekends. I drove six hours home each Friday, and another six hours back to work each Sunday. This difficult situation lasted for an entire year. But our commitment to living in small town America was so fierce, we wouldn't even consider relocating even as our friends increasingly questioned our sanity. Many didn't understand why we would willingly "starve" to live the small town lifestyle.

As time passed, we created more concrete personal and financial goals for ourselves. When we created goals and our lives became more focused, our income and enjoy of life increased. Twenty years after our move, we are better off financially than many of our friends. In addition, we are stronger as a couple because we weathered, together, those tougher financial and emotional times. It's been a long, hard road to travel. However, we wouldn't trade our experience for a million dollars. We have survived the toughest of times and know the future can't be any harder than the past. We have no regrets.

To us, living the small town lifestyle is worth the sacrifices we made early in our move. We are able to connect to something bigger than ourselves. We have a deep realization that we're enjoying all that life has to offer. All of this is due to the ability to slow down and take a mental break in this fast-paced world in which we live. The small town lifestyle provides to ability to turn off the cell phone and take a leisurely stroll along a grassy pathway in the middle of a lush green forest.

Do Whatever it Takes

When it comes to achieving your goals, knowing what you should do is usually the easiest step; the remaining steps are the hard ones. However, once you know what you need to do, the next step is to get out into the world and do it. The only question remaining is: Do you have the courage?

Courage is taking an action you know you must do in order to accomplish a goal. It's about repeatedly stepping outside of your comfort zone until you can take that step with confidence. Countless examples of courage can be found everyday in our Armed Forces. These men and women know they must perform tasks that are sometimes outside of their comfort zones. I'm sure the first time an Army Special Forces Ranger parachutes from an airplane, there is a brief moment of being outside his comfort zone, but he keeps doing it until he is ranked among the elite of our fighting forces.

You and I can tap into this outstanding quality we call courage. Of course, the line between courage and foolishness is a thin one. Take it from someone who knows. For this reason, I strongly suggest that you do not quit your job and venture out to pursue your small town dream in the middle of a blizzard.

A more reasonable course of action in pursuit of your goal is to build the courage to follow your small town dream by learning everything you can about your chosen path. These four fundamental steps constitute a strategy that will help you get started:

Four Fundamental Steps You Must Take Before Moving to Small Town America

#1: Create a Family Policy Statement

#2. Research Your Goals

#3: Get Your Financial House in Order

#4: Eliminate Your Financial Past

Create a Family Policy Statement

The happiest moments of my life have been the few which I have passed at home in the bosom of my family.
~ Thomas Jefferson ~

The first step to living your small town dream is to create a Family Policy Statement (FPS). Creating a family policy statement is much like creating an investment policy statement. Like with an investment statement, the family policy or mission statement would include your objectives, your time horizon and even your risk tolerance. Those with a lower risk tolerance may want to temper risk by seeking to take their current job with them to a new location, like through the option of telecommuting, or may seek a similar profession in the new location. For others, achieving the "dream" may involve taking the plunge of creating an entirely new way of making a living.

Your FPS would include the following:

- Timeline for moving to the small town of your choice
- Complete list of your sources of income today (Salary, real estate income, dividend income, etc.)
- Complete list of your sources of income after you move
- A list of small towns for consideration
- A detailed definition of why you want to move to a small town

Answer the question: "If I knew I were going to die a year from today, what would I want to accomplish?" and you've begun the process of creating your Family Policy Statement.

Achieving the small-town dream means first defining that dream. You need to understand what your goal is and why you want to achieve it before you'll be able to take the necessary steps (and be comfortable with the level of risk) it'll take to get there.

Remember: any major move involves a transition period that includes an element of mourning what you've left behind. You'll likely be leaving behind good friends and much of what is familiar. Even the process of finding a new dentist, a favorite grocery store, a reliable mechanic can feel overwhelming at first, even a little bit sad, for we don't realize how much the daily encounters with people whose paths frequently cross ours make up the fabrics of our lives until we need to start anew.

Weaving together a new and even better dream needs to start with a vision of the finished product and an inventory of necessary materials.

How are great accomplishments achieved? You weigh potential benefits of various courses of action against potential costs. There is a secret to making the right choice every time. It's in determining what will take you closer to your lifetime goal, those things you "must" accomplish. It's in defining what you want to achieve in life, no matter what it takes.

To many, the small town lifestyle seems to appear out of reach. To that I ask, "How badly do you want it?" Only you can answer that question. But time and time again, history has shown that people who know what they want and focus on their goals have achieved success more often than not—and technology and economic reality has made this a better time to make this kind of leap than perhaps anytime in history.

One of the benefits of being human has always been is ability to choose among many opportunities that present themselves each day because somebody made a choice. At the end of your life, would you rather say, "I'm glad I did? " Or "I wish I would have?"

> *Take calculated risks. That is quite different from being rash.*
> *~ George Patton ~*

The process of creating a family policy statement helps you understand the "why" of making the move and thus determine whether the end goal is worth the risk. You and your family should be in complete agreement. Some people even involve extended family members or friends in the process. Their support can sometimes make or break a decision, and their knowledge and contacts may be invaluable as you choose a new home and launch a new business.

One local couple started the process by listing cities they thought would appeal to them, then asking like-minded friends and family members if they knew of others. The couple endured some good-natured ribbing at the thoroughness of their process. Friends said things like, "How about Podunk. We've heard that's a nice place!" But the end result? They explored some of the nation's most attractive small cities, picked one that best fit their criteria and couldn't be happier with the end result.

Once you complete the family policy statement, everyone should sign it. You're then ready to launch your adventure with the whole crew on board. You and your family must be in complete agreement. You need to involve your spouse, your children, etc., in your decision-making process. Would it be worth quitting your job, giving up on your pension, and relocating today? In many cases, probably not.

But once you complete your FPS, every member of your family should sign it. This will ensure everyone affected by the move will know when, where, and why the family is moving. A blank Family Policy Statement is provided on the following page for your use.

Small Town Dream – The Guide to Moving to Small Town America

Family Policy Statement

Your time horizon for moving to Small Town America:

_____

Your reasons for moving to Small Town America:

_____

_____

Your sources of income today:

Salary: _____

Amount: _____

Real estate rental income:

_____

Amount: _____

Dividend income:

_____

Amount: _____

Royalty income:

_____

Amount: _____

Small Town Dream – The Guide to Moving to Small Town America

Interest income:
_____

Amount: _____

Your sources of income after you move:

Salary: _____

Amount: _____

Real estate rental income:
_____

Amount: _____

Dividend income:
_____

Amount: _____

Royalty income:
_____

Amount: _____

Interest income:
_____

Amount: _____

List here the small towns or region you would like to move. Small towns or regions in which you are considering a move (list):

_____

_____

_____

_____

_____

_____

_____

_____

Small Town Dream – The Guide to Moving to Small Town America

Why do you want to move to a specific area?:

_____

_____

What will you do for income once you move?:

_____

_____

_____

Signature: _____ Date: /   /

Signature: _____ Date: /   /

Signature: _____ Date: /   /

Signature: _____ Date: /   /

Signature: _____ Date: /   /

Signature: _____ Date: /   /

Small Town Dream – The Guide to Moving to Small Town America

Now that you have completed your Family Policy Statement, make a photocopy and distribute it to everyone who signed it. This will accomplish two vital elements.

1. First, it helps everyone to understand the goal you and your family are striving to achieve. That goal is your Small town Dream.

1. Second, it helps everyone understand why your current lifestyle may change. When your daughter asks why you gave her $10 to go to the mall instead of the usual $20, you can remind her of your FPS. This will create a goal that the entire family wants to accomplish together.

Focus: It's the Reason Why You Set Goals

Since much of the rest of this book contains strategies to help fund your dream of living in a small town, we need to take a moment to review why we set goals. It wasn't until I was 27 that I began to understand the true meaning of goals. Since the age of 13, I have been very goal-oriented. I accomplished many of my goals; I also fell miserably short of others.

To truly benefit from your goals, you need to understand why you are striving toward them. When I was 20, I set a goal of having million dollars by age 22. Unfortunately, this was only a vague wish. Did I want the million dollars? No! A million dollars is only a stack of currency and coins. I wanted what the million dollars would give me. It would give me the freedom to live my live the way I wanted to live it. It would allow me to spend time with my family. It would allow me to travel the world.

Instead of the goal of a million dollars, my goal should have been to achieve a specific lifestyle for my family and myself. Regardless of the goal, the "why" behind the goal is more vital than the goal itself. The "why" will keep you believing in your dream when nobody else wants to listen to you. It will motivate you to get up early and work late.

It will keep you on track during the darkest hours. It is up to you to decide what that end goal will be. Once you decide what your end game is, you need to build the lifestyle to support that goal.

Research Your Goals

There is one quality which one must possess to win, and that is definiteness of purpose, the knowledge of what one wants, and a burning desire to possess it.
~ Napoleon Hill ~

Since moving to a small town is one of your lifetime goals, it is likely that you already know at least a little bit about the area of your dreams. Even so, living in a small town is different than visiting for a weekend. Before you uproot your family and change your lifestyle, you need to lay a careful foundation so you can build a successful future. You want to gather facts and make informed decisions. When you chose a new place to live, you want to think like a resident, not a tourist. Here are 15 strategies that will help you "go native:"

Fifteen Strategies to Smooth Your Transition and Validate Your Family Policy Statement

Each of these steps will help you make progress toward your Small Town Dream. They lay the groundwork for the achievement of your ultimate goal.

I. Talk to People Who Share Your Goals

One of the first steps to take when selecting a new community is to ask other families about their favorite small town or rural locations. This will help you connect with people who have similar tastes and may provide insight on communities you may not have otherwise known about or considered.

II. Talk to Local Merchants

The local merchants usually know a lot about the potential of the area. Ask for their insight about community politics, trends, etc. By talking with the local storeowners, you'll gain insight into the growth potential of the area. For example, you probably wouldn't want to purchase property in a town that is expected to decline in population because the largest employer in the town is expected to close in two months. Understanding the community is vital to your happiness.

III. Learn About the Job Market

While subscribing to the local newspaper and visiting the newspapers website will give you valuable insight into the type of jobs available and the average pay scale, a visit to the local Chamber of Commerce can provide a wealth of information about the local business environment.

Even if you are not interested in joining the chamber, this information will give you insight into the type of businesses in the community. For example, if the majority of the members are logging companies, you'll know what type of employment may be immediately available.

When you visit the Chamber of Commerce, you'll want to know two things:

- Is the membership of the chamber is increasing or decreasing?
- What types of companies are members?

If the membership of the chamber has been decreasing over the past several years, this may indicate a shrinking population. Also, if you know what type of companies are members, it will give you insight into whether or not the town is overly dependent on a single industry.

For example, in that logging town we previously mentioned, what will happen to the town once the timber is gone? Insight into the town's economic base will give you a valuable peek at possible future developments in your destination of choice.

IV. Talk with Local Real Estate Agents

Local real estate agents are a qualified group of professionals to talk with about a community. These professionals can usually provide insight into future growth patterns, real estate prices, and what is likely to happen in a town over the next several years.

V. Contact the Newcomers Club and Research Local Meetup Groups in the Area.

The Newcomers club is an organization provided in many communities to welcome new residents. Ask them to send you a welcome package. This package usually contains discount coupons from local businesses.

Visit the website Meetup.com. This is a website in which anyone can create a group for those with similar interests. For example, countless groups exist across America from knitting, jogging, bitcoin and blockchain related and more. Look for the type of Meetup groups in your target region and town you are looking to move it. You'll discover what types of groups are available and how active they are.

Attending Meetup groups is also a great way to meet a number of people in your new hometown in a short period of time, too.

VI. Contact the Local School System

If you have children, this is extremely important. Inform the school system that you will be making a move in the near future and would like them to send you an information package. Also, make sure to find out about the graduation rate, the student/teacher ratio at various grade levels; enrichment programs or tutoring opportunities; style of instruction; how parents are involved as volunteers and more.

VII. Subscribe to the Local Newspaper

Once you select the area or town you would like to eventually move to, subscribe to the local newspaper including the online version. This will give you insight into the community. Before Jennifer and I moved to Northern Michigan in the early 1990's, we subscribed to the local newspaper of our destination community.

This allowed us to read about the area before we committed ourselves to moving. The newspaper provided first-hand information about area employment and insight into real estate prices. It also gives you a real feel for the community and what it values.

VIII. Visit Your Selected Destination Throughout the Year

After you have narrowed your choices to two or three locations, you should visit them at various times throughout the year. Make it a point to take a trip during the busy times as well as the off-season. By visiting your potential choices throughout the year, you will have a better understanding of whether or not an annual "boom-bust" cycle exists.

For example, some towns have enormous numbers of visitors during the summer and winter months. However, during spring and fall it seems that every business in that town shuts down. By understanding the "boom-bust" cycle, you'll know which of the local services are available for year-round use.

IX. Consider the Weather Patterns

Become familiar with the year-round weather patterns of your future community. Visitors to the warm beaches of Northern Michigan should be familiar with what being in the "snowbelt" actually means, just as winter tourists in Florida enjoying the cooler months of the year may want to know what a town is like in mid-August.

X. Consider the Travel Distance to Your Family and Friends

The number of family get-togethers you are able to attend may be greatly diminished—or enhanced—if you move to your small town of choice. Travel distance and cost may play an important role in the final decision for your move.

XI. Visit the Local Medical Facility

Studies have revealed that people are staying healthier longer. However, should you require medical attention,
it is always a good idea to be familiar with the local hospitals and medical care facilities.

XII. Senior Activities

No matter what your age when you relocate to a new town, you should review the senior activities and community events offered. Whether or not you or a family member currently plan to use these facilities, you should plan for the future before it arrives. It may someday be important for a surviving spouse or elderly family member to know the depth and breadth of available activities.

XIII. Visit the Planning Department of City Hall

Visit the planning department and ask to see the master plan of the city. The master plan outlines the development direction for the city's future. The master plan is public information and provides a great way to get an understanding of what the city officials want for their community in coming years.

XIV. Don't Buy into a Community Based on a Rumor

Don't buy into a community because someone informed you about a potential multi-million dollar development. You should never invest money purely on rumor. The community you select should provide you with what you want and need to live the lifestyle you desire. Purchase into the community because of what it currently has and not what it may have in 5-to-10 years.

XV. Consider Buying Your Dream Property Now

Many families purchase their property several years before they actually move. This allows them to pay off some of the mortgage and to get their home ready before they actually move.

These 15 steps are meant to create momentum for your dream. Remember, "A rolling stone gathers no moss." By implementing the above steps, you are slowly turning the wheels in your favor. These steps help you gather vital information about your future community. In some instances, the area you initially decided to move to may not be right for your family. It may not provide adequate after-school activities, or the hospital may be too far away for comfort. Remember you are making a move to a small town to enjoy the area, not to increase your stress level, so make your decision based on solid facts. Revise and refine your Family Policy Statement if necessary based on your findings.

Paying for Your Dream

__When I chased after money, I never had enough. When I got my life on purpose and focused on giving of myself and everything that arrived into my life, then I was prosperous.__
~ Wayne Dyer ~

My job in the financial services arena gave me the opportunity to travel the state of Michigan and beyond. When I traveled, I met numerous people. I met them on the airplanes as I fly to and from Cherry Capital Airport in Traverse City. I met them in restaurants and office meeting rooms. Many of these occasional visitors to the region, most of them tourists drawn by the natural beauty and recreational amenities, dream of moving to the area permanently.

Once people learn I actually live around in Northern Michigan, they ask the same question: "How are you able to live and work in Northern Michigan?" That's usually followed by something to the effect of: "I can't earn the same amount of money in a town like this as I can in a city. How do you earn a permanent living?"

If my wife Jennifer and I can make the move, anyone can. Napoleon Hill, the author of the great book Think and Grow Rich wrote, "Anything the mind can conceive and believe it can achieve." That is the motto of the Small Town Dream.

If you can conceive and believe that you can move to a small town in Northern Michigan or elsewhere, you can achieve it. However, the lack of high-paying employment opportunities has hindered many from making the move and is one reason why many are only able to enjoy the area on a part-time basis.

Living in a relatively rural community can be hard. The trials and tribulations of our early days Up North caused Jennifer and me to struggle. We had to take second jobs and be more creative with our finances. But we also learned to enjoy life fully. We were and are able to spend hours on the beach or walking the shops in nearby towns on a lazy Saturday afternoon.

Unlike when Jennifer and I moved to the area, numerous income opportunities now exist in Northern Michigan, and our beautiful region is not unique. Smart people are looking for more balanced lives, and smart companies and business opportunities are following.

At the time we moved, a popular local saying was *"A view of the bay is worth half the pay."*

We can attest to the validity of that slogan. However, 20 years after our move, the local saying is *"A view of the bay is worth more today."* The employment opportunities offered around where we live have increased dramatically over the years.

The explosion of new employers has driven wages higher and the increased popularity of the region has created additional business opportunities for entrepreneurs.

Should you move your family to a small town (or any town) without a job or source of income? Of course not! Should you carefully craft a plan to create an income stream that will enable you to move? Yes!

Every strategy is this book has been used to help fund our Small Town Dream. The programs outlined here allow Jennifer to work from home. Our goal was to design a lifestyle that allows us to enjoy our time as we desire. Are we millionaires? No! But having a million dollars is not our goal.

We want the freedom to spend our time working, traveling, or relaxing on the beach. We don't want to be controlled by a clock on the wall. Besides, a million dollars would not be enough to achieve and maintain this lifestyle. Since we don't have the million anyway, we don't focus on a single dollar figure, we focus on cash flow.

Money should be used to fund your lifestyle; it should not be an end goal. If you spend your precious time chasing the goal of having a million dollars, you can easily forget why you are working so hard. I don't want you to fall into the trap many others have. I want you to enjoy a beautiful sunset from your very own piece of paradise.

Consider that when most people set a goal of moving to the small town of their dreams, they ask themselves the following question, "How much money do I need before I make the move?" If, for example, your goal is to have one million dollars in your bank account, you then have to ask yourself, "Will it be enough?" Let's look at the numbers. If you have one million dollars the day you move to a small town, how much income will that produce? The income produced by your assets should support your lifestyle. You can't afford to siphon off principal just to live.

Let's assume your million dollars will produce an annual return of 6 percent. In this example, your million dollars will produce $60,000 in annual cash flow.

$1,000,000 x 6% = $60,000
(Remember, you will not siphon off principal to support your lifestyle.)

Is that enough money to support your lifestyle? Only you can answer that question. However, what happens to your dream if you don't achieve your million-dollar goal? The simple answer is, you won't make the move. Your dream will end in quiet desperation. No matter how much you want to live in Northern Michigan, the million-dollar goal has tripped you up. Your calculations are based on having a million dollars prior to your move, not in creating a lifestyle. That is why you need to create a cash flow requirement rather than a bank account size.

Cash flow is what determines your lifestyle, not net worth. I know many people who own several cars, three boats, and two houses. The asset side of their net worth indicates $750,000. However, when they factor in the liability side and calculate their true net worth, they have a negative $250,000. They simply own hundreds of thousands of dollars of "stuff."

What is "stuff?" Stuff is two boats, four snowmobiles, two sets of golf clubs and two BMW's. While owning them can be fun, you need to determine if your Small Town Dream requires them. Many people who own multiple piles of "stuff" must work just to keep a roof over their heads. They need to work 80 hours a week to pay for all the "stuff."

Many of them are so busy working they can't enjoy their "stuff" to the fullest. Although it appears they have everything, they lack the free cash flow to keep the wheels of their life rotating smoothly.

One of the greatest secrets that I learned from being in the financial services industry is that living in a big house doesn't make you rich. Many people falsely believe that someone who lives in a 5,000 square foot house overlooking the ocean or a golf course is rich. The truth is, some of these families have trouble making their monthly mortgage payments.

Many "cash flow-orientated" individuals have no desire to live in a 5,000 square foot house and own seven cars. They have a different mindset. Cash flow-orientated people want to own a nice house, pay for the necessities of life and enjoy their free time. They chose how they want to produce a cash flow from their job, the assets they own or both.

A Lifestyle or a Job…It's Your Choice

Anyone can move to a small town and "earn a living." However, if you want to design a lifestyle, you need a plan. There is a big difference between earning a living and designing a lifestyle. Designing a lifestyle is not better than earning a living, nor is earning a living better than designing a lifestyle. They are just different. It is up to you to decide how you want to spend your time, talent and skills. However, my goal is to assist you in designing the lifestyle of your dreams.

A lifestyle allows you to enjoy life on your terms. It allows you to enjoy long walks on the beach, playing early-morning golf and spending countless hours skiing through the powder-white snow offered by the local ski resorts. A lifestyle gives you the free time to truly enjoy everything our nation's most beautiful regions have to offer.

Earning a living is exactly what it sounds like. You work to pay your bills. You work nights, weekends and any other shift to keep your family fed and gas in the car. Free time is a scarce resource. It doesn't matter how much money you make, anyone can be in the "earning a living" group. I know families that earn over $150,000 per year and still have a difficult time paying their bills. I once knew an individual who earned $50,000 in one month and declared bankruptcy the same month. The "earning a living" crowd always has "too much month left at the end of the money". They live from paycheck to paycheck. They have the best cars, live in the best neighborhoods and yet are cash poor.

To realize your Small Town Dream to the fullest, you will want to convert your frame of mind. Begin to design a lifestyle instead of just earning a living.

During a recent conversation, my wife Jennifer was talking with a school employee about the upcoming school year. During the conversation, the school employee made an interesting comment. The comment was that the number of school children usually declined between the beginning and end of the school year.

The employee said she didn't know why this happened and couldn't offer a reasonable explanation. After my wife and I discussed this comment, and I reflected upon my several years of selling real estate, we came to the following conclusion.

Many families move to a small town during the summer months. The kids are out of school and the weather is mild. Many times, the big city house is sold and the proceeds are used to purchase a large home in a "nice" neighborhood. In most instances, the move itself is simple and eventless.

However, within a few short months, the newly transplanted family feels the need to own a boat. Of course, a new boat would allow them to truly enjoy the region's many lakes. After a few more months, the husband needs a snowmobile, and the wife needs a new car. Soon the free cash flow begins to shrink as the monthly payments increase.

Within a few short years there is a heavy debt burden and the thoughts of moving back to the city creep in. This may be due to poor household budgeting and the lack of a plan prior to the move. Unfortunately, this happened to several couples we met over the years. The deadly cycle of cash-in, cash-out began in earnest.

Despite these experiences, opportunity abounds. Anyone can "earn a living," but if you want to truly enjoy your Small Town lifestyle, your financial affairs need to be in order.

Once you've made the decision to move to a small town, you need to create a solid cash flow to fund your dream. Two vital steps in solidifying your future include learning how to create a cash flow statement and a household budget.

A cash flow statement is your first step. This financial statement shows you where your money is coming from (cash inflow) and where it is going (cash outflow). Once you have created a cash flow statement, you'll learn how create a household budget. Your budget will allocate your money to its highest and best use.

The best way to create a cash flow statement is to record three months of your spending history, and compile this information in a cash flow statement. You will need to categorize your spending under specific headings. For example, under the heading of "personal care" on your cash flow statement, you could combine haircuts, shampoo, and cologne into one amount. This will allow you to simplify your statement.

Let's look at a sample cash flow statement for a hypothetical couple, John and Mary Smith. The Smiths' monthly cash flow statement begins on the following page.

Small Town Dream – The Guide to Moving to Small Town America

Monthly Cash Flow Statement

For the Month of: September

Cash Inflow (Net)
Bonus
Dividends
Interest
Other income
Rental income
Net salary (Husband) $3,450.00
Net salary (Wife) $850.00

Total Monthly Income $4,300.00

Cash Outflow

General Expense
Auto maintenance/repair $86.00
Auto payments $764.00
Clothing $164.00
Credit card payments $170.00
Daycare $300.00
Entertainment $100.00
Gasoline $175.00
Tithe to church $60.00

Food Expense
Dining out $440.00
Groceries $340.00

Miscellaneous (candy bars, etc.) $50.00

House Expense
Maintenance $60.00
Mortgage $760.00
Rent payment
Monthly tax amount $125.00

Insurance (monthly)
Auto $150.00
Health $194.00
House $50.00
Life $39.00

Utilities
Electric $60.00
Natural gas $75.00
Telephone $65.00
Water $45.00

Total Monthly Outflow $4,272.00

Total Surplus (Deficit) $28.00

As you can determine from the Smith's September cash flow statement, they have $28 remaining at the end of the month. I have included a blank cash flow statement for your use:

Small Town Dream – The Guide to Moving to Small Town America

Monthly Cash Flow Statement

For the Month of: _____

Cash Inflow (Net)

Bonus _____

Dividends _____

Interest _____

Other income _____

Rental income _____

Net salary (Husband) _____

Net salary (Wife) _____

Total Monthly Income _____

Cash Outflow

General Expense

Auto maintenance/repair _____

Auto payments _____

Clothing _____

Credit card payments _____

Daycare _____

Entertainment _____

Gasoline _____

Tithe to church _____

Food Expense

Dining out _____

Groceries _____

Miscellaneous (candy bars, etc.) _____

House Expense

Maintenance _____

Mortgage/rent _____

Monthly tax amount _____

Insurance (monthly)

Auto _____

Health _____

House _____

Life _____

Utilities

Electric _____

Natural gas _____

Telephone _____

Water _____

Total Monthly Outflow _____

Total Surplus (Deficit) _____

Now that you know the status of your cash flow, you need to create a monthly budget and get the remainder of your financial house in order.

Create a Monthly Budget Allocation

A comprehensive budget will allow you to channel your financial resources toward your Small Town Dream. Without a budget, vast amounts of money may slip through your fingers and your dreams of living in a new community may not come true. Many people think they don't make enough money to create a budget.

However, people who earn at least $25,000 per year will have over a million dollars pass through their hands over their working lifetimes. This is a tremendous amount of money.

The chart below demonstrates how much money an individual may earn over an average working lifetime until retirement:

Years Until Retirement	Yearly Income	Lifetime Income
40	$25,000	$1,000,000
30	$50,000	$1,500,000
20	$85,000	$1,700,000

As you can see, an individual making $25,000 per year will earn $1,000,000 over a 40-year career. That is a substantial amount of money passing this individual's way. To approximate how much money will pass your way in your lifetime, use the formula below:

Years Until Retirement x Yearly Income = Lifetime Income

_____ X _____ = _____

Many people who initially use the above formula are astonished with the amount of money they might earn over their working lifetime. After you determine how much money will be coming your way, doesn't it make sense to try to keep and invest as much of it as possible?

Once you have determined how much money you will earn, the next step is to determine how much money you will make prior to your move. I call this amount Small Town Cash. This is the amount of cash you will have to begin funding your dreams. This gives you a definite goal for the amount of money that you will need to save before your move. By knowing your Small Town Cash number it will make it easier to eliminate the $3.50 daily Mocha Latte from your budget.

Number of years until your move x Yearly Savings = Small Town Cash

_____ X _____ = _____

Monthly Transaction Record Sheets

To keep track of your cash flow, record your expenses on a Monthly Transaction Record Sheet. Think of this sheet as a financial diary. First you write down a description of any purchases and the amount spent, then indicate if you paid cash, wrote a check or used a credit card. By recording how you paid for the transaction and what you bought, you will track how and where you spend money.

To get a good sampling, use this method for at least three months. Even better is a year's worth of records. This method is designed
to give you an accurate and true picture of your spending habits. I have included a sample Monthly Transaction Record for our hypothetical couple, John and Mary Smith. The Smiths want to move their family to a small town in four years, so they have decided to start planning.

Small Town Dream – The Guide to Moving to Small Town America

The first step they took was to begin recording their purchases on a Monthly Transaction Record Sheet. Both John and Mary used a Transaction Record Sheet for three months. Once the three-month period was over, they combined their results into one sheet. The following is a sampling from the combined Transaction Record Sheet for the Smiths:

Monthly Transaction Record Sheet

For the Month of: July

Date	Description of Transaction	Amount	Cash	Check	Credit Card
7/1	Groceries	$25.00	X		
7/1	Gasoline for car	$12.00	X		
7/1	Kid's clothes	$74.00			X
7/2	Candy bar at work	$.65	X		
7/2	New pair of shoes	$57.00		X	
7/6	Lunch at deli	$13.48			X
7/6	Dinner out	$29.77			X
7/6	New shirt & pants	$85.64			X
7/10	New couch	$780.00			X
7/15	Car repairs- Brakes	$412.00			X
7/15	Paid credit card bill	$170.00		X	
7/15	Paid day care bill	$325.00		X	
7/15	Diapers/baby formula	$89.54		X	
7/15	Tithe to church	$30.00	X		
7/20	Dinner out with kids	$79.71			X
7/25	New cordless tools	$250.00			X

Small Town Dream – The Guide to Moving to Small Town America

The sample of the Smith's expenses demonstrates how quickly a family's income can seem to evaporate. Note the $.65 spent on candy. If you are going to keep an accurate record of your expenses, no expense should be overlooked regardless of size.

Monthly Transaction Record Sheets

The first time my wife Jennifer and I completed and reviewed our Monthly Transaction Record Sheets, we were amazed at how much money slipped through our fingers. For example, we bought snacks and soft drinks and ate lunch at one of the local restaurants on a daily basis.

Without realizing it, we were spending 15 percent of our monthly take-home income on frivolous items. By using a Monthly Transaction Record Sheet, we were able to see how we were spending our money and began to take control of our finances. Monthly Transaction Record Sheet

For the Month of: _____

Date   Description of Transaction   Amount   Cash   Check   Credit Card

_____

_____

_____

_____

_____

_____

_____

_____

Another great way to keep track of your daily transactions is to use a spreadsheet on your computer of a budgeting app on your phone. Simply search the Google Pay store for budgeting apps.

Just input your spending information at the end of each day. The app/spreadsheet will keep track of all your purchases and automatically enable you to add them up quickly at the end of three months.

Once you have completed Monthly Transaction Sheets for a period of three months, you will have enough information about your spending habits to develop a monthly budget.

The purpose of a budget is to redirect any portion of your income that is currently slipping through your fingers into your bank account. Remember, your budget will include all of your category headings on your monthly transaction worksheets.

However, before you begin to set budget amounts in each category, you should make sure to create a line item called the "Down Payment for Dream Property."

The "Down Payment for Dream Property" account is to be used to purchase property in your small town of choice. It doesn't matter if you save $5 or $50 a week. The purpose of this account is to provide a portion of the funds you will need to make your move. Your Small Town Dream begins now!

Create an Emergency Fund

The second line item you need to add to your household budget is "Emergency Fund." An emergency fund is another vital element to building your financial future. Many financial planners say a family should stash away at least six months of expenses into an emergency fund. However, three to four months of expenses should be sufficient for families with a steady income stream. If your income is erratic, closer to six months of expenses may be better for your situation. An emergency fund is an excellent source of cash if you have an unexpected financial requirement once you move.

The first step in creating an emergency fund is to add the heading to your monthly budget. The account should be funded on a monthly basis, just like any other expense. Once you have three or more months of expenses in this account, you will stop funding it.

Should you run into an emergency prior to funding your emergency account, here are five suggestions for how to obtain money in a relatively short amount of time:

1. Overdraft Protection

Place overdraft protection on your checking account. Overdraft protection prevents a check from being returned for non-sufficient funds. Overdraft protection is a loan made by the bank to you should you accidentally write a check greater than the funds in your checking account. The overdraft loan from the bank is usually paid back in monthly installments.

2. Establish a Line of Credit

An open line of credit, also known as a signature loan, is an unsecured loan that has already been approved by the bank. To open a line of credit, you need to visit your local bank and complete the necessary paperwork.

3. Use Secured Loans

A secured loan is a loan secured by another asset. For example, if you have a $1,000.00 certificate of deposit (CD), you could obtain a loan for approximately $1,000.00 by using your CD as collateral.

4. Tap Your Home Equity

If you are a homeowner or already own property in the small town to which you're planning a move, consider obtaining a home equity loan that offers check-writing privileges. It's a great way to have funds available for an emergency. A home equity loan amount is usually 75 to 80 percent of the value of your home, less what you currently owe on the home. You need to fill out all of the home equity paperwork with the bank or mortgage company. Once everything is complete, the bank can give you a checkbook instead of a lump sum for your monetary needs. By having check writing privileges, you can write checks for any amount up to the pre-determined limit. The interest for this type of loan may also be tax deductible. Check with your tax advisor.

5. Credit Card Cash Advances

Use this option only as a last resort and ONLY after you have exhausted all other options including the possibility of borrowing money from family and friends. The unfavorable interest rates on most cash advances make this option cost prohibitive. However, you should be familiar with how credit card cash advances work.

Monitor Your Progress

Once you have organized your household finances into an easy-to-follow format, you will need to monitor your progress continually. One of the best ways is to use an annual net worth statement. Your net worth is what you own reduced by what you owe. The formula for net worth is:

Total Assets - Total Liabilities = Net Worth

For example, if you have $50,000.00 in assets and $45,000.00 in liabilities your net worth is $5,000.00. Assets are cash, real estate, personal property, etc. A liability is any outstanding debt.

Since most people would not liquidate 100% of their assets to pay off their liabilities, calculating your net worth is a "textbook" type of exercise, but it serves to provide an indication of the direction of your financial progress. The best time to do your net worth statement is in December or January. During this time of year most people are creating goals for the coming year. In fact, a great New Year's resolution is to increase your net worth by 10 percent each year. I have included a blank net worth statement on the following pages for your use.

Small Town Dream – The Guide to Moving to Small Town America

Net Worth Statement

Date: /   /

Assets

Liquid Assets (Short-term Assets)
Checking account: $_____

Cash value of life insurance policy _____

Money market account: _____

Savings account: _____

Household Assets (Long-term Assets)
Antiques: $_____

Automobile #1:   _____

Automobile #2:   _____

Clothes: _____

Dishes: _____

Furniture: _____

Home computer system: _____

Home entertainment center: _____

House: _____

Jewelry: _____

Other real estate holdings: _____

Recreational vehicles: (boats, jet skis, snowmobiles, etc.) _____

Tools: _____

Investment and Retirement Assets (Long-term Assets)

Bonds: $_____

Company retirement plan #1: _____

Company retirement plan #2: _____

Individual retirement account #1: _____

Individual retirement account #2: _____

Mutual funds: _____

Stocks: _____

Other: _____

Small Town Dream – The Guide to Moving to Small Town America

Total Assets (Short-term Assets + Long-term Assets)

$_____

Liabilities

Short-term Liabilities (Paid off in 3 years or less)

Automobile loan #1: $_____

Automobile loan #2:   _____

Credit card payments: _____

Medical bills: _____

Student loans: _____

Long-term Liabilities

Home mortgage: $_____

Notes payable: _____

Other real estate loans: _____

Total Liabilities (Short-term Liabilities + Long-term Liabilities)

$_____

Net Worth (Total Assets – Total Liabilities)

$_____

In addition to an annual net worth statement, you should also create an annual Cash Flow Statement (simply a summary of your monthly cash flow statements). This annual Cash Flow Statement allows you to make any necessary changes to your budget. For example, at the end of December you may realize that you are not budgeting enough throughout the year for your holiday expenses.

Eliminate Your Financial Past

Can I pay my Visa payment with my MasterCard?
~ Author Unknown ~

Credit card debt is a national dilemma and the most cunning adversary to securing your financial future. Many credit card companies use enticing promotions to lure consumers into using credit cards by increasing credit limits and offering pre-approved credit cards with great introductory rates. All of these offers are an attempt to install the habit of spending now and paying later.

Unfortunately, most people don't realize how destructive this habit is until their credit card payments become the largest part of their monthly budget. Credit card debt, as a percentage of income, has been on the rise for the past two decades. No matter how difficult it may be to break the habit of credit card debt, the reward is worth the effort.

One debt reducing strategy is what I call "The Debt Elimination Pyramid." By using this debt elimination strategy, you will be able to completely pay off your credit card balances and get started on the road to securing your financial future.

The Debt Elimination Pyramid

The Debt Elimination Pyramid is designed to help you pay off your credit card balances as quickly and painlessly as possible. For example, if you wanted to tear down a pyramid, where would you start? The most logical place to start is at the tip of the pyramid, since the foundation is so tremendous.

You would begin at the top of the pyramid and remove one brick at a time until the entire pyramid had been torn down. That is the same method you will follow to remove all of your credit card balances. Credit card debt is destroyed one payment at a time.

There are four simple steps in the Debt Elimination Pyramid.

1. Write down all of your credit card outstanding balances in ascending order (smallest to largest). For example, if you have four different credit cards, all with outstanding balances, you will write down the lowest to the highest balance on a sheet of paper. This is referred to as your **Debt Pyramid**.

2. Concentrate on completely paying off the card with the lowest balance.

By paying off your lowest credit card balance, you eliminate the tip of your debt pyramid. You will pay as much as you can financially afford over and above the minimum payment required. For example, if the minimum monthly payment is $40 on your smallest balance, you could write a check for $75 ($40 minimum required plus an additional $35). You pay this extra amount every month until the entire balance of the first card is paid off.

3. Once the first credit card is completely paid off, concentrate on the next tier.

After you have completely paid off the credit card balance at the tip of your pyramid, you will add the minimum monthly payment of your first card to the minimum monthly payment of your second smallest credit card. For example, if the minimum payment for your first position credit card was $40 and the payment for the second position card is $55, then your monthly payment to the second credit card will be $95 ($40 +$55 = $95). Just as you did with the first credit card, you are now eliminating the balance of the second card at a faster pace than you would if you just paid the minimum monthly amount required. In addition, the original total minimum payment requirement was already allocated into your budget. Thus, you will not need to allocate any additional money to pay off your total debt. This step of the strategy will decrease the time required to reduce your overall credit card balance.

4. Repeat steps one through three until all of your credit cards are completely paid off.

For example, a hypothetical couple, Kim and Don Sanders, are using the Debt Elimination Pyramid Strategy to pay off their credit card debt. They have seven credit cards with total monthly combined payments of $855. Their outstanding balance is $27,500. They want to eliminate their credit card debt completely.

The first step Kim and Don took was to write down the outstanding balances of each credit card in ascending order. They also included the minimum monthly payment requirement for each credit card.

Here is what Don and Kim Sanders' Debt Pyramid looks like:

Debt Elimination Pyramid Worksheet (See the Debt Pyramid below)

Credit Card Name	Outstanding Balance	Minimum Payment
Credit card #1	$1,575.00	$85.00
Credit card #2	$1,900.00	$110.00
Credit card #3	$2,374.00	$165.00
Credit card #4	$2,596.00	$130.00
Credit card #5	$3,750.00	$240.00
Credit card #6	$10,551.00	$295.00

Use the Debt Elimination Pyramid worksheet on the following page to write down your current outstanding credit card balances in ascending order.

Small Town Dream – The Guide to Moving to Small Town America

Debt Elimination Pyramid Worksheet

Credit Card Name	Outstanding Balance	Minimum Payment
_____	$_____	$_____
_____	$_____	$_____
_____	$_____	$_____
_____	$_____	$_____
_____	$_____	$_____
_____	$_____	$_____
_____	$_____	$_____
_____	$_____	$_____

Now that you have created your own pyramid, follow the four steps in the Debt Elimination Pyramid Strategy to eliminate your credit card debt completely.

Another popular debt elimination approach many people follow is to pay off the credit card charging the highest rate of interest first. Once this card is paid off, they pay off the next highest interest rate. On the surface, this may seem like the best approach. However, when reviewing all the factors involved, it may be the toughest to follow.

While it is true that, by using either method, you are decreasing the total amount of time you are carrying balances on your credit card by making monthly payments over and above the minimum requirement, the length of time required to pay off a large balance can be frustrating to many people.

By using my method, you receive an enormous psychological benefit each time one of your cards gets paid off. You will feel that you have torn off the top of the pyramid and can see the light at the end of your tunnel of debt. This alone can be enough encouragement to last you throughout the process of breaking the chains of debt.

How to Stop Using Your Credit Cards

Once you begin conquering your credit card balances, the worst thing to do is to begin using the cards again. Here are four approaches to help you stop using your credit cards:

1. Lock Up or Cut Up Your Credit Cards

The best way to stop using your credit cards is not to carry them. Once your debts are paid, eliminate all but one of your credit cards. The card you keep is for emergency use only, since there may be times when you will need to have access to a large amount of purchasing power on short notice. For example, you may need to replace the engine in your car or buy an airplane ticket in a family emergency. An innovative way to remember that your credit card is for emergency use only is to tape a piece of paper to your credit card with the words: "FOR EMERGENCY USE ONLY."

2. Write Checks

Get in the habit of writing checks for all of your purchases. This offers two advantages. The first benefit is that you can't make a purchase unless you have the money in your checking account. This may eliminate frivolous spending. The second advantage is that you will get out of the habit of using your credit cards.

3. Use Debit Cards

If you don't like writing checks, get a debit card. A debit card is similar to a credit card with one distinct difference. Whenever you make a purchase with a debit card, the money is immediately subtracted from your checking account. You cannot spend more than you have in your bank account. Make sure to write down your spending in your check register!

4. Reward Yourself When You Pay Off a Credit Card

Every time you pay off an outstanding balance, treat yourself to a long walk or a dinner out.

How to Make Money in a Small Town

You have to do what you love to do, not get stuck in that comfort zone of a regular job. Life is not a dress rehearsal. This is it.
~ Lucinda Basset ~

The following ways to make money—anywhere—are broad-based strategies, not all-inclusive solutions. Jennifer and I have used each of the six items to fund our lifestyle since we moved to Northern Michigan.

- Find a job in your small town of choice
- Freelance
- Buy real estate
- Become a road warrior
- Create a website and sell stuff (affiliate marketing)
- Start a business

Each strategy offers a unique set of trials and tribulations. One strategy is not better than any other. If a strategy is not working to your satisfaction, you can change direction almost instantly.

A. Find an Existing Job

This strategy is the easiest to implement. This is the route many families use when they first move to a new small town. In fact, this is how Jennifer and I kept food on the table when we first moved in 1992.

You may need to take this path, too. The greatest benefit from getting a job is that it will allow you to pay your bills and establish roots in your newly adopted community.

Finding a job gives you an instant income and an immediate sphere of influence. Certainly the income from your job is vital; however, the people you work with everyday are also important. Since a small town, by nature, is small both geographically and in total population, the people you work with today are the very same you'll see for years to come at the grocery store and beaches. Here are a few suggestions for beginning your job hunt.

- Subscribe to the Local Newspaper or other Local Publications
    - This will provide insight to the type of employment available.

- Search the Internet
    - Several employment websites are available to assist you in searching for small town employment. One of the best ways to locate these sites is to use the search terms: "small town employment" or "jobs" coupled with the name of your town or county of choice.

- Contact Temporary Agencies
    - Temporary agencies can provide immediate employment at the area's best companies.

- Targeted Search
    - If you want to remain in the same industry in which you are currently employed, submit your resume to similar companies. Unfortunately, many of the top jobs are usually not advertised in the newspaper. These top-paying positions are often filled by word-of-mouth rather than job postings.

One of the best ways to locate companies in your current profession is to review the local chamber of commerce website. Once you have created a list of organizations, you can either email them your resume or get in your car and personally drop off your resume to the Human Resource department of each firm. This gives you the opportunity to sell yourself to your potential employer.

If you want to change careers, your move to a small town may provide you the opportunity to pursue your desired line of work. What is your desired line of work?

Only you can answer that question. Listen to your inner voice. This is the small voice in your heart that was becoming faint and distant, drowned out by the noise of life. Revisit this voice and listen for it during your silent and relaxing moments.

In addition to listening to your inner voice, ask your parents or other family members how you spent your time in your younger years. This will give you an opportunity to discover your calling.

For example, if you enjoyed writing poems and short stories when you were younger, consider becoming a staff writer for a small town newspaper. If you enjoyed building models, look into becoming a licensed builder.

Consider your current hobbies and how they may help you earn an income. There are many artisans, writers, instructors, etc. that are creating an income from their previous hobbies.

The Career Action Plan Worksheet provided on the following page may help you determine the direction of your new career:

Small Town Dream – The Guide to Moving to Small Town America

Career Action Plan Worksheet

What is my current job or career?

_____

What do I enjoy about my current job/career?

_____

_____

What do I dislike about my current job/career?

_____

_____

Why am I considering changing my job/career?

_____

_____

What activities did I enjoy when I was younger?

_____

_____

Write a short description of the benefits you would enjoy in your new career:

_____

_____

_____

Small Town Success Story

I recently met a man, Tim, formerly from large suburban town in Michigan. His father owns a house on the shores of Torch Lake in Northern Michigan. During a visit to his father's house in 2009, Tim and his wife JoAnn made the decision to move to the small town on the lake at which they'd long vacationed.

They were enjoying a glass of lemonade on his father's deck watching the sun set over the crystal clear waters. As the sun slowly dove toward the tree-lined hills, Tim jokingly asked JoAnn if she would be interested in moving to this area permanently.

After a few moments of laughter, they began to discuss the idea seriously. And after following the Targeted Search strategy outlined earlier in the chapter, Tim had several job offers within a couple of weeks of hand delivering his resume. They now live in Northern Michigan, full-time.

B. Freelance

Thanks to the Internet, freelancing has never been easier. Within a few moments anyone can obtain a listing of freelance opportunities. Many companies have embraced the power of the Internet and post assignments online. No matter what your profession or skill level, you can probably find multiple freelance opportunities. Here is a brief list of categories available for freelancing:

- Accounting
- Copyright law
- Creative writing
- Database design and development
- Engineering
- Personal financial planning

- Graphic design
- Medical billing
- Personal assistant
- Public relations
- Sales
- Travel planning
- Web site development and design

Here are a few sites to offer your services:

- Guru.com
- Fiverr.com
- 99designs.com
- Elance
- Upwork.com

C. Real Estate – Rental Real Estate and Vacant Land

I. Real Estate - Rental Real Estate

Many opportunities exist in the area of rental real estate. The main goal for owning rental real estate should be a positive monthly cash flow. The tax benefits provided by real estate should be secondary. I have met many real estate investors over the years that purchase rental property with a negative monthly cash flow hoping the tax benefits would provide a positive return at year-end. A real estate investment should not be a drain on your cash flow. I believe the sole purpose of rental real estate is to put money into your bank account.

The reason I personally dislike rental property with a negative cash flow is the possibility that I may lose the property to foreclosure if I don't have the money in my bank account to meet the required monthly payment. Your objective in buying property isn't to fund the bank foreclosure department. Prior to purchasing rental property, consult a real estate professional familiar with all aspects of investment real estate.

In addition to the positive cash flow, consider any additional benefits to owning a specific piece of real estate. For example, I own a week of timeshare at a Northern Michigan resort. It provides me the benefit of positive cash flow and waterfront enjoyment. The resort is responsible for renting my unit and maintenance. Once the resort deducts its property management fee, it sends a check for the remaining balance.

Over the past several years, this property has been rented five out of the seven nights available. Thus, I am able to use the remaining nights to enjoy a few relaxing evenings on prime waterfront real estate, and still make a profit.

II. Real Estate - Vacant Land

Several years ago we purchased a lot on Old Mission Peninsula near Traverse City in Northern Michigan. The lot was located about 10 miles out on the peninsula and had shared water access. We purchased the lot for approximately $22,500 and sold it a year later for a profit. This was our introduction to land speculation in Northern Michigan. When I look back, I should have kept the property in my portfolio. However, at the time I needed the cash to support my lifestyle.

One of the drawbacks of owning vacant land is the drain on your cash flow. Vacant land doesn't usually produce a cash flow, thus your income must support the monthly debt service. However, here are three suggestions you can use to produce a positive cash flow from your vacant land portfolio.

1. Subdivide Acreage Parcels

Subdividing acreage parcels may be an excellent way to generate cash. For example, a friend recently purchased a 10-acre parcel for $45,000. He paid $4,500 as a down payment and financed the remaining $40,500. The bank immediately appraised the property at $48,000. The day he closed on the property, he had a $3,000 profit. He then divided the 10-acre parcel into four 2.5 acreage parcels. After consulting with a local real estate professional, he decided to sell the four parcels. The asking prices range from $28,900 to $35,900. The price for each parcel is very competitive with the surrounding property.

Once he sells all of the parcels, this transaction will generate a $65,000-plus profit after all costs of sale. Prior to dividing any acreage parcel, consult a real estate professional and the local governmental office to determine if any restrictions exist against subdividing.

2. Timber the Property

If you own (or have the chance to purchase) a heavily wooded parcel, consider selling the timber. This will provide immediate cash flow. When timbering, you must work with a high-quality logging company. Consider working with a timbering firm that "select cuts," harvesting only some of the trees on your property. This process usually allows your property to maintain its health and general appearance. Consult a reputable logging firm and competent attorney prior to timbering your property.

3. Sell the Mineral Rights

If you own the mineral rights of the property, consider selling them. This will provide you a monthly cash flow to support the property's debt service. Although it is hard to find property with mineral rights, some still are available. Consult a reputable geologist and a competent attorney prior to selling your mineral rights.

D. Become a Road Warrior - Obtain a Traveling Job

I was a road warrior from 1998 until 2009 as a mutual fund, annuity and separate account wholesaler. I traveled 4-5 days a week. I traveled 12 months out of the year.

For those 10 years, I flew over 75,000 airline miles each year from the Cherry Capital Airport in Traverse City. Fortunately, my schedule changed dramatically in 2009 and I was able to stop traveling and spending more time with my family and running my businesses. During my travels, I met many fellow road warriors.

I met a businessman who lives part-time in two small towns in Northern Michigan. He lives on Mackinac Island in Northern Michigan during the summer months and in Gaylord, more in the center of the state of Michigan, in the winter. John travels the United States and beyond due to his consulting practice. He logs over 150,000 airline miles per year and says he loves every minute of it. When he is not traveling, he is able to conduct business via conference calls and the Internet. Many traveling jobs exist; you only need to determine if you would enjoy the traveling lifestyle.

Many jobs requiring travel provide a very good income. This helps to offset the disadvantage of being away from your family during the week. Before accepting a job that requires travel, consult your spouse and/or family. Some couples simply don't want to be apart no matter what the reward.

An alternative to living full-time in a small town and traveling during the week is to live in a city during the week and a small town on the weekends. A couple we know, Tony and Beth, enjoy this lifestyle. Tony works in the construction trade and lives in a major city in Michigan during the week. He drives back to see the family for the weekend to the small Northern Michigan town in which his wife Beth lives full-time and raises their two children. When I asked Tony and Beth if they enjoy this type of lifestyle, here were their answers:

Tony: *"I usually work 60-70 hours per week. Before we moved to Northern Michigan, I would leave for work before my sons woke up and I returned home after they were in bed. Beth worked, too. Beth and I would see each other a few minutes in the evening and few moments each morning. I also worked most weekends. We decided to move to a small town, and it was the best move we ever made. I don't work on the weekends because all of my jobs are downstate. I am finally able to spend a few days each week of quality time with my wife and kids."*

Beth: *"I knew living apart wouldn't be easy; it has made us appreciate what we have. We have great kids and a wonderful life. We are able to spend quality time with them and each other. We made the decision to live the lifestyle we wanted. Before we moved, I rarely saw Tony during the week anyway, so not much has changed. I would be sleeping when he left for work in the morning and working when he returned in the evening. Now we get to spend weekends together and get to raise our kids in a small town. It is something we won't change for anything."*

E. Sell Stuff Online – Affiliate Marketing

More and more families are enjoying the freedom and flexibility of lifestyle by using affiliate marketing. Affiliate marketing is when you earn a commission by promoting other people's products or services on your website. You simply find products or services you like and promote it to earn an affiliate commission for each sale you're your make. If you are interested in learning more how you can earn additional income with affiliate marketing, check out our website at LearnFromHome.com to learn about our complete training programs.

A friend of mine was able to quit his job at a Fortune 500 company and move to small town by becoming an affiliate marketer. Working as an affiliate may provide an additional source of income for you to enjoy your small town dream, too.

F. Start a Business

Owning your own business can be the best or worst experience you will ever have. It can be the best because it can give you the freedom you need to spend quality time with your family and to earn a good income. However, to be successful in your own business, you must make a commitment of time, energy and resources. In addition to these commitments, you must have the desire to succeed. No amount of time or money will ensure success. The only insurance you have against failure is a burning desire to succeed. If you have a burning desire, setbacks won't deter you.

Statistics remind us that many small businesses are destined to fail. In fact, studies have shown that nine out of 10 businesses fail. When I read those statistics, I know that if I want to ensure success, I may have to start 10 businesses. If you want to succeed in business, you must increase your odds of success. To stack the odds in your favor, market a product or service that is in high demand. Of course, every entrepreneur wants to have a successful business selling a "hot" product. To identify potentially "hot" products, consider the major trends in society. By studying these trends, you will begin to "see the future" and build a company to cater to a future demand. There are many ways to predict the future.

One of the best ways to learn about upcoming trends is to read articles from many different industries. By reading articles from unrelated industries, you begin to see an early groundswell for a particular product or service. For example, I believe there are three main trends that will affect society over the next 30 years: health care including natural home remedies, technology including cryptocurrencies, blockchain and the internet, and financial services including financial planning, tax planning and personal money management.

While there are many independent factors influencing these sectors, the main underpinning forces behind these three trends are the baby boom generation and the millennials. The baby boomers have always influenced the marketplace. Members of this generation were born between 1946 and 1964. This generation is the most powerful the world has ever experienced. They are the wealthiest and healthiest group yet. This powerful force will have enormous influence on the products and services over the next 30 years.

The millennials are the most tech savoy generation yet. This generation is comfortable looking to the internet for assistance and don't necessary need to meet face-to-face to follow professional recommendations. They are also open to taking online learning classes, too.

Consider these trends when starting your business:

Health-Related Products and Services

The demand for high quality health-related products and services is tremendous. The baby boomers are redefining retirement and are enjoying life on their own terms. They will remain active for decades longer than their parents did. Due to longer life expectancies, the boomers will demand innovative products and services to support their active lifestyles. This will create a tremendous opportunity for forward-looking entrepreneurs. Although it may be difficult to start a biotechnology company researching human DNA mapping, you have countless numbers of other potential businesses you can start to cater to this need. The millennials are also interested in the same areas, too.

One area to consider is the marketing of superfruit and vegetable-based dietary supplements, organic and nature-based products. I believe this is an explosive industry in the near future. Multinational corporations are already positioning themselves to take advantage of this rapidly expanding market.

To capitalize on this trend, Jennifer and I founded Traverse Bay Farms in 2001 to market and distribute super fruit and fruit-based products. Our product line includes Fruit Advantage super fruit supplements, tart cherry juice concentrate, organic preserves, dried fruit (including dried cherries, dried blueberries and more), fruit-based salsas and fruit-based barbecue sauces.

In fact, since 2009, our Traverse Bay Farms fruit and gourmet salsas has won 26+ national food awards including 18 Scovie Awards. Traverse Bay Farms is the #1 nationally award winning super fruit brand in America.

Our experience may offer an excellent opportunity for others to build a similar business in the healthy products and healthy eating category.

To assist others, we have developed a step-by-step program others can use to start their own healthy products business. If you are interested in this category, you can learn more on our Traverse Bay Farms website at www.traversebayfarms.com.

We offer a wholesale, retail, dropship and an affiliate program. Our opportunity is designed to offer a jump-start to those interested in starting a health-related business. This unique opportunity is outlined at www.traversebayfarms.com

Financial Services

The greatest transfer of wealth in the history of the United States will occur within the next few decades. This "money-in-motion" will create a tremendous demand for competent professionals. A few professions that will likely experience high growth during the next few decades include estate planning attorneys, real estate professional, financial advisors, insurance professionals, and accountants. In addition to these professions, opportunities may exist for high quality finance-related services and publications. These include educational seminars, books, and online personal finance universities. If you are interested in the financial services area, begin your study today and position yourself for the explosive growth of tomorrow.

Technology-Related Services

The "dot com" boom and bust of the late 1990s was only an introduction to the technology frenzy that may occur over the next several decades. Today, cryptocurrencies and blockchain technology is the next generation of technology that will move our world forward. Anything that is related to cryptocurrencies, blockchain and Fintech will be the buzz words for the next several years.

Today's technology allows you to conduct meetings via the Internet using a satellite connection while fishing two miles off shore. If you are interested in starting a technology-related company, focus on the development of products and services catering to individual freedom and flexibility. Also, focus on blockchain and fintech related technology.

Start an Internet Business

The Internet makes it possible for anyone to earn a full-time living "online." I know of an Internet entrepreneur who earns more than $120,000 each month selling electronic books. Is there a secret to succeeding online? No! Like any other business model, a successful Internet venture must implement proven strategies and techniques. There are five areas to should consider when building your Internet empire.

1. Select a target market
2. Define your site
3. Select a domain name
4. Build your website
5. Create a strategic marketing plan

I. Select a Target Market

What is your target market? What need does your Internet business satisfy? Will your site sell everything from gas grills to walking shoes? Will you specialize in servicing a select niche market? Who is the target market for your business? Determining who your customers are is the most vital decision you can make about any business venture.

II. Define Your Site

Once you have defined your target market, how will you define your site? When defining your site, you must be creative, you must "think outside of the box". Thinking outside of the box will give you a tremendous advantage over your competition. Most of your competitors are not creative thinkers. They fall into this trap by narrowly defining their web sites. The broader the definition you create for your site, the broader your potential target market will be.

Defining your site within a narrow spectrum will place you at a disadvantage. Let me explain what I mean. For example, if you own a retirement planning site, you could easily define your site as the following: "My site is a retirement planning site."

That is a good definition for any retirement planning site; however, that definition will limit your thinking on future advertising campaigns. With the current definition, you may decide only to advertise on finance-related sites and in financial web rings. However, if you define your retirement planning site as: "My site not only helps people prepare for retirement, it also teaches personal finance strategies," you expand your promotional opportunities and customer base.

The latter definition opens the door to a broader market. Since personal finance strategies are a natural subset of retirement planning, you would include these types of strategies on your site. This broader definition is thinking outside of the box. Here are a few niche ideas to help you get started with a money-related site:

Investment-Related Sites
Stocks, bonds, mutual funds, etc.

Personal Finance Sites
Basic household money management and budgeting sites.

Credit Card Sites
Since your retirement planning site includes personal finance strategies, it could also include information on teaching people how to use credit card debt wisely.

Life Insurance Sites

Since your retirement planning site includes personal finance strategies, it probably would include information on basic life insurance strategies.

As you can see, just by giving your site a broader definition, you instantly increase the number of customers and way to advertise.

III. Select a Domain Name

Now that you have selected a target market for your business and defined your website, you need a domain name. A domain name is your unique address on the web. Just as in real estate, where each property has a unique address, each web site has a unique cyberspace address.

Here are four tips to use when selecting a domain name for your online business:

1. Your domain name should reflect the content of your site. For example, if you want to create an online casino, you won't want the domain name www.bartendertraining.com. You would want the domain www.youronlinecasino.com.
2. Your domain name needs to be catchy and easy to remember. For example, www.etaxplanning.com is a great example of an easy to remember name. It also tells what your site is about.
3. Your domain name must be easy to spell: www.orchardofhealth.com
4. Select a short domain name. However, today it is very difficult to obtain a short domain name. Thus, when selecting a domain name for your online business, try to select a descriptive and easy to spell and remember domain name.

The domain extension is a vital part of your domain name. The most common extensions in the Unites States are .com, .net, or .org. Below is a list for the proposed purposes for each extension:

.com to be used for for-profit business

.net to be used for an internet/network related business

.org to be used for a not-for-profit business

In addition to the above, dozens of new extensions have been, and will be, created to keep up with domain demand. The cost to register a domain may vary from $10 to $15 per name. Check out Godaddy.com and Hostgator.com to learn more about purchasing a domain name. Finally, check out the site LearnFromHome.com for complete step-by-step online training in a number of different areas including starting an online business.

IV. Build Your Website

The Internet has brought the entire world together in a way that never existed before. In addition to globalizing your business, you can usually create a web presence within a few hours.

Several programs exist that can easily create a professional website for your Internet business. You can build your site using Wordpress or simply use a complete end-to-end ecommerce solution like Shopify.com To sort through the various programs and find the one best suited for your needs, here are a few suggestions:

- Conduct an internet searching using the following phrases:
    - Start an ecommerce business
    - Learn about Shopify
    - Learn Wordpress

This will help to get you started on your online venture.

V. Create a Strategic Marketing Campaign

We have all heard the secret to succeeding in real estate is the three L's: location, location, location." To succeed on the Internet you need traffic. Without traffic, you're done! Period.

It doesn't matter if you have the best-designed site on the web. It doesn't matter if you're offering the highest quality products at the lowest prices. It doesn't matter if you provide the best customer service. Nothing matters without a huge number of "eyeballs" viewing your site. Until you have a huge number of visitors to your site, you will only make small amounts of money.

Thus, the first logical step is to create an advertising and marketing plan. A comprehensive plan should drive traffic to your site and will probably increase your income.

Your plan can be as simple as a one-page handwritten overview or a 100-page computer generated presentation. The choice is yours, but whatever you do, you must have a written plan. The following is a brief example of what a successful advertising and marketing plan should contain. Feel free to use the outline as a model for your own plan.

Advertising and Promotion Strategies

It is extremely difficult to succeed on the Internet with only an online marketing campaign. Many Internet companies are creating strategic marketing promotions that include both online and offline campaigns. The following marketing strategies will help you get started:

A. Create a strategic alliance list. To locate sites that offer complimentary products, conduct a keyword search on any of the major search engines. Once you have compiled a list of potential websites, contact the owners and webmasters of these sites and suggest a strategic alliance.

B. Purchase ads in email lists to advertise your business.

C. Create a reciprocal links campaign with your strategic partners. Place your strategic partner's link on your site and yours on their site.

D. Search engine marketing. You can use organic and paid-advertising. Organic search marketing is coding your page to target certain keywords. Paid advertising is paying Google and Yahoo and the other search engines to place your ads.

E. Write press releases about your products and submit them to press release services. A well placed press release can results in thousands of dollars in business.

F. Contact a writer of the business section at your local newspaper and ask him/her to write an article about your online business. Many writers are searching for compelling and inspiring content. Your story may be just what they need.

G. Be a guest speaker on your local radio station. Many talk-radio hosts are searching for guests to appear on their shows. I have used call-in radio talk shows to promote my businesses.

H. Be a guest speaker on your local television station. I have made television guest appearances for years for my businesses.

I. Create a Linkin.com profile. This is an excellent way to network with other professionals.

J. Create your own YouTube Channel. Video is the most popular way to get free traffic and evergreen exposure.

While the purpose of this book isn't to provide you with a complete marketing plan to launch your new website, use the steps above to get started.

Getting Ready to Move to Your Small Town

Don't ever let anyone steal your dreams.
~ Dexter Yager ~

Building relations is vital to your success in any endeavor. Because your destination of choice—a small town—is by definition small in population and geographical distance, it makes sense to begin building your relationships prior to your move. Here is a list of relationships you need to start building today:

A. Banking Relationships

Banking relationships are extremely important. You'll need services from checking accounts and savings accounts to personal loans and mortgages. Open a checking or savings account with a local bank. After you open the account, make an appointment with the bank manager. Inform the manager you will be moving Small town in the near future and want to build relationships with local business professionals. The benefit of having this face-to-face meeting is to introduce yourself to the individual who could lend you money in the future.

B. Real Estate Professionals

The majority of real estate professionals are knowledgeable and insightful. Contact a real estate office, and ask to speak with the sales manager. Inform the sales manager that you will be moving to the area in the near future and would like to work with an agent who can teach you about the area. You'll probably be referred to an outstanding agent who will be willing to assist you with all of your real estate needs.

C. Investment Professionals

Once you move, you may chose to move your investment accounts closer to your new home. Contact several investment professionals and inform them that you will be moving to the area. Tell each of them that you will be transferring your assets to a financial planner in their region. Interview several financial advisors to learn about their services and determine your comfort level. Your relationship with your investment advisor is one of the most important you'll have. A long distance advisor relationship isn't necessarily bad, but face-to-face meetings are extremely important when discussing your finances.

D. Residential Builders and Contractors

If you decide to build your Small Town Dream house, you will need to work with an experienced builder. During the construction process, you'll spend countless hours discussing your plans with your builder. It would be wise to select your builder prior to your move.

Small Town Dream – The Guide to Moving to Small Town America

A Road Map for Success

Getting your professional relationships in order is just one of the steps that will help you prepare for your move. Here is an activity list to help guide you. Use it as a timetable to complete your short, intermediate, and long-term small town goals.

Small Town Preparation List

Planning Your Foundation: These are your ultra short-term goals. These goals should be completed within 2–4 weeks of finishing this book.

Building Your Foundation: Your short-term goals should be completed within 1–6 months.

Constructing Your Dream: These goals should be started and completed within 6–36 months.

Enjoying Your Dream: Should be enjoyed after 36-plus months.

Here is a sample of a completed Small Town Preparation List. After you review the sample below, you'll have a better idea of the types of activities that could be placed on your list.

Small Town Dream – The Guide to Moving to Small Town America

Below is the outline for Matt and Beth Anderson. They both enjoy snowmobiling. They have spent numerous winter weekends riding the snowmobile trails in their favorite small town. They want to start building their small town dream by purchasing 10 acres of vacant property near the snowmobile trails. Here is their completed outline:

Pre-Move Preparation List for Matt and Beth Anderson

Planning Your Foundation: (completed within 2-4 weeks)
- Complete a Family Policy Statement
- Subscribe to local newspapers in areas to which you're considering a move.

Building Your Foundation: (completed within 1-6 months)
- Contact the local Chamber of Commerce
- Research communities in surrounding counties
- Contact a real estate professional and begin to view properties
- Contact a small town bank and open a checking account

Constructing Your Dream: (completed within 6-36 months)
- Purchase a 10-acre parcel of real estate near the snowmobile trails
- Start a home-based business

Enjoying Your Dream: (completed after 36 months)
Move and start enjoying their Small Town Dream

Small Town Dream – The Guide to Moving to Small Town America

The Small Town Activity worksheet provided on the following page will guide you in your Small Town adventure:

Small Town Pre-Move Activity List for: (Insert Your Names Below)
_____

Planning Your Foundation: Date Completed
_____   _____

_____   _____

Building Your Foundation: Date Completed
_____   _____

_____   _____

Constructing Your Dream: Date Completed
_____   _____

_____   _____

Enjoying Your Dream: Date Completed
_____   _____

_____   _____

10½ Step Small Town Dream Checklist

What To Do Now #1: Create a goals list. Sit down with your family and determine if moving to a small town is appropriate. Your goals list will determine if you and your family should even consider moving. Take your time and make sure you have considered all aspects of moving to a smaller community.

What To Do Now #2: Complete the Family Policy Statement (FPS). Make sure all family members are in agreement on making the move. Once it is completed, have all family members sign and date the FPS.

What To Do Now #3: Begin to familiarize yourself with the many great small town communities in the region of your choice. Take multiple three-day weekend trips to several different towns. Experience first hand the small town lifestyle. This will help you decide if the region to which you're drawn is an appropriate full-time home for you and your family.

What To Do Now #4: Get your financial house in order. Begin using daily transaction sheets. Once you have completed three months, compile this information into a budget, and construct a net worth statement. Do this on a monthly and an annual basis.

What To Do Now #5: Begin to pay off any outstanding credit card debt. Follow the Debt Elimination Pyramid strategy. Once you are debt free, you will be free to invest for your future, rather than paying for your past.

What To Do Now #6: Consider purchasing your property today! The best way to begin your search is to use a real estate professional. This will allow you to keep your finger on the pulse of the region's real estate. Contact a local real estate company and begin to inquire about property values and property options.

What To Do Now #7: Start your business. Most small businesses lose money in the first few years of operations. Consider starting your new business prior to your move. This will allow time to build your profits.

What To Do Now #8: Consolidate all of your IRAs and brokerage accounts. By bringing all of your accounts under one umbrella, you may lower or completely eliminate any annual fees the mutual fund or brokerage companies charge, putting more money into your pocket now. Consolidating your accounts allows you to keep better track of your investments.

What To Do Now #9: Begin building your small town relationships today. Contact several real estate, financial, mortgage, builders, and bank professionals and inform them that you are considering moving to the area. This will allow you to build relationships prior to your permanent move

What To Do Now #10: Update your resume. Once you have updated your resume, create a list of companies that you would like to work for and send your resume to each of them. Personally contact each company within one week of submitting your resume to follow-up on your mailing.

What To Do Now #10 ½: Any other activity not mentioned on this checklist.

Small Town Dream – The Guide to Moving to Small Town America

10 ½ Step Small town Dream Checklist

TASK COMPLETED   YES   NO

What To Do Now #1:   ____   ____
Date Completed: _____

What To Do Now #2:   ____   ____
Date Completed: _____

What To Do Now #3:   ____   ____
Date Completed: _____

What To Do Now #4:   ____   ____
Date Completed: _____

What To Do Now #5:   ____   ____
Date Completed: _____

What To Do Now #6:   ____   ____
Date Completed: _____

What To Do Now #7:   ____   ____
Date Completed: _____

What To Do Now #8:   ____   ____
Date Completed: _____

What To Do Now #9:   ____   ____
Date Completed: _____

What To Do Now #10: _____   _____

Date Completed: _____

What To Do Now # 10 ½: _____   _____

Date Completed: _____

Small Town Dream – The Guide to Moving to Small Town America

Contact List

Use the blank form below to help you to keep track of the professionals you'll need to get started with your Small Town Dream

Real Estate Professionals I Will Contact:

_____
_____
_____

_____

Builders and Contractors I Will Contact:

_____
_____
_____

_____

Investment Advisors I Will Contact:

_____
_____
_____

_____

Bank Professionals I Will Contact:

_____
_____
_____

_____

Conclusion

This book has offered definitions and information regarding many different aspects of personal finance and moving to a small town. It is not recommended that you uproot your family and move without careful pre-planning. Use the educational information in this book to follow your dreams.

By following the information offered here, and personalizing the worksheets, charts, etc., you are well on your way to reaching your financial goals and maybe even your ultimate Small Town Dream. Thank you for reading this book. I began this book with the following quote and I would like to leave you with it, too:

"Live your dreams and believe in yourself. That is the only way to the top."
~ Andrew LaPointe ~

Notes

Notes